Talks about Mauritania
in a high-school courtyard

Mouhamed Lemine Ould El Kettab

Talks about Mauritania in a high-school courtyard

Drawings and scenes
Mohamed El Hacen

© L'Harmattan, 2011
5-7, rue de l'Ecole-Polytechnique, 75005 Paris

http://www.librairieharmattan.com
diffusion.harmattan@wanadoo.fr
harmattan1@wanadoo.fr

ISBN : 978-2-296-54635-6
EAN : 9782296546356

CONTENTS

PRESENTATION 7

NAJIB 11

NAJIB PRESENTS NOUAKCHOTT 15

KADIA PRESENTS GORGOL 21

SIDATY PRESENTS ASSABA 27

ISSELMOU PRESENTS TAGANT 33

DIAGNA PRESENTS GUIDIMAGHA 39

SOULEIMANE PRESENTS TRARZA 45

BILAL PRESENTS BRAKNA 51

MARIEME PRESENTS HODH EL GHARBI 55

MOULAYE PRESENTS HODH ECHERGUI 61

HOURIA PRESENTS INCHIRI 67

GUEJMOUL PRESENTS TIRIS-ZEMOUR 73

SAFIA PRESENTS DAKHLET NOUADHIBOU 79

MOUSTAPHA PRESENTS ADRAR 85

HAMMADI PRESENTS MAURITANIA 93

Présentation

Ce travail accompli en langue anglaise et intitulé :

Causerie sur la Mauritanie dans la cour d'un lycée décrit une situation imaginaire où les élèves d'une classe de seconde du Lycée National, assistés de leur professeur d'anglais, décident, à l'initiative de l'un d'entre eux, d'organiser dans la cour du lycée des causeries au cours desquelles des élèves présentent des exposés suivis de débats sur les wilayas dont ils sont originaires.

Bien que ce travail comporte une technique narrative, des personnages bien différenciés, un héros omniprésent et un dialogue soutenu, éléments caractéristiques du genre romanesque, il n'est pas pour autant une œuvre de fiction cherchant primordialement à conforter l'imagination et à susciter une émotion esthétique visée comme but en soi. Il a plutôt un objectif didactique et informatif, dans la mesure où, à travers les exposés présentés par les élèves, à travers celui, plus global de leur professeur, et à travers les interrogations et les commentaires qu'ils ont inspirés aux élèves, il vise à :

- Situer géographiquement chacune des wilayas mauritaniennes ;
- Mettre en exergue de façon succincte leurs ressources, leurs potentialités et leurs vocations économiques respectives ;

- Mettre un accent particulier sur le caractère exotique et la vocation touristique des wilayas qui représentent de telles spécificités ;
- Evoquer les atouts particuliers de chaque wilaya ;
- Indiquer les difficultés et les handicaps de nature à freiner les efforts du développement au niveau de chaque wilaya ;
- Indexer les pratiques sociales néfastes tels que le divorce abusif, le gavage des jeunes filles, la polygamie, le mariage précoce, la paresse etc. ainsi que les comportements irresponsables comme la dégradation du milieu écologique, la destruction de la biodiversité, les gaspillages inconsidérés etc. ;
- Faire ressortir les efforts déployés par les pouvoirs publics dans les domaines de la santé, de l'éducation, de l'alphabétisation, de la lutte contre la pauvreté et la promotion socioculturelle, à travers l'intégration de la femme et l'instauration de l'obligation de la scolarisation etc. ;
- Souligner la crédibilité grandissante dont jouit la Mauritanie depuis la mise en place en 1986 de profondes réformes politiques et économiques qui se sont traduites par l'instauration du libéralisme économique, de la démocratie multipartite, de l'État de droit et des libertés fondamentales.

[2]Tels sont les objectifs que ce travail vise à atteindre. Il y a lieu par ailleurs de souligner qu'il pourrait aussi servir à plusieurs usages, en particulier :

- Servir de texte de lecture individuelle ou collective pour les élèves et les étudiants mauritaniens, texte qui présente l'avantage d'être centré sur les réalités des Mauritaniens et leurs préoccupations de tous les jours ;

- Contribuer à faire connaître aux étrangers les caractéristiques, les potentialités et les atouts de la Mauritanie ainsi que les réalisations économiques, politiques et socioculturelles qui y ont été accomplies.

Ce travail est donc de nature à familiariser la jeunesse mauritanienne avec les multiples facettes de la réalité nationale et à aider à faire connaître davantage la Mauritanie au plan international.

NAJIB

Najib was a 15 year-old boy, born in Nouakchott to a university professor and his wife, a medical doctor, who lived in a house of their own where they had settled in the early 1980s. That house was located in a nameless street of the residential quarter of Travagh Zeina. Najib was a fair-complexioned, good-looking youngster with wide black eyes, an aquiline nose and raven black silky hair. He was well mannered, soft-spoken, sharp-minded and methodical. He liked reading, listening to music and watching cultural television programs. He was also fond of fine arts such as painting, sculpture, ballet, cinema and drama. Najib attended a nameless junior high-school located in the vicinity of his home. In June, 2000 he passed with brio the entrance exam for the first year of senior high-school; he was since then looking forward to attend the time-honored senior high-school called "lycée national" where a significant section of the national elite had its secondary education.

On October the 1st, 2000, at 8'oclock, Najib proceeded to the lycée national with a mixture of joy and nervousness. In the lycée, he sought and found the board on which the lists of the admitted pupils' sere posted. New pupils flocked around the board attempting to spot their names on the placarded lists. Najib met some of his new class-mates; as they introduced themselves to one another, new comers joined in, and the circle they formed kept widening. Their talks hinged on the different schools they had attended, the difficulties they had encountered during their exams and the specificities of the various regions of the country they had come from. They also exchanged questions and ideas about the new curriculum ushered in by the new reform of the education system that has just come into force. Most pupils expressed their happiness vis-à-vis the prospect of having to study foreign languages as they consider that absolutely indispensable for a modern and really qualifying education. As the pupils extensively evoked their past experiences in the variegated schools they had attended, and as they described vividly the different aspects of life in the various regions of the country they belong to, it dawned upon Najib that it would be instructive for all and asundery that pupils who were willing to talk to their class-mates about their Wilayas do so, be it in a sketchy manner for that would allow everybody to learn a great deal about the different Mauritanian Wilayas. He suggested that idea to his class-mates who adopted it enthusiastically. it was finally agreed that once the courses flag off, they, the first year pupils, will be using after-school times to gather under one of the trees in the schoolyard in order to exchange information on their respective regions giving thereby every one of them the opportunity to learn as much as possible about the multifaceted reality of the country. The pupils contemplated this experience with a great deal of excitement and decided to inform their English teacher of this initiative of theirs; and he for his part, promised to partake of such an experience.

NAJIB PRESENTS NOUAKCHOTT

On October the 12th, 2000 at 5 p.m. when they finished their last lesson of the day, the first year pupils gathered as planned under one of the trees of the schoolyard with the English teacher attending.

Najib took the floor to say:

"Good after-noon ladies and gentlemen. Allow me first of all to introduce myself to those of you I haven't met as yet. My name is Najib. I am from Nouakchott. I am glad to have met you all and I am proud to be your class-mate. To start with, let me on your behalf thank our English teacher, mister Hammadi, who has kindly accepted to attend these brainstorming sessions we've decided to organize. Thank you sir for being with us. We have, as you all know, decided to hold every other Thursday an informal get-together during our after-school times in order to exchange information concerning our home Wilayas and eventually to talk about our experiences and to discuss anything which is of interest to us. I am sure we'll find this unprecedented experience very stimulating indeed! I am willing to be the first speaker. I shall, if you don't mind, tell you some words about my birth place and home town, Nouakchott. And subsequently I'll call upon some one of you to volunteer to talk about the Wilaya he or she comes from at our next get-together. Does everybody agree on this proposition?"

Many voices said in unison: "yes, everybody does! So you may start Najib, we're listening!"

After a little cough to clear his voice, Najib said:

"all right, you know, when we consider now the mushrooming city of Nouakchott with its numerous streets full of traffic and pedestrians going in all directions we can hardly imagine that in 1957, that is to say, some 44 years ago, this city consisted solely in half a dozen banco houses built around a well located on the number 1 trans African road that used to link Dakar to Algiers. The main building of that hamlet was a garage where the Lorries that used to ply that road were fixed whenever they needed repair. Those Lorries belonged to a transportation company called 'Lacombe'. All around that tiny village was wilderness nothing but wilderness! I saw pictures of that village and I had opportunity to watch a TV program on it and believe you me, it resembled a small dot lost in an endless wild bushy landscape. It looked so fragile and so unreal that one could hardly imagine it expanding into a big town and a capital city at that! And yet that was what happened. In 1959, it was decided, as you probably know, to transfer the political capital of Mauritania from Saint Louis of Senegal to that Lilliputian village which was turned into the fledgling capital of our country. Thus the seeds of Nouakchott were sown as it were. Indeed some buildings were hastily constructed to accommodate the presidency, the national assembly and the different ministries.

In that same year the territorial assembly proclaimed the birth of the Islamic Republic of Mauritania which acceded to national independence, as you all know, on November the 28th, 1960. The first meetings of the cabinet were held under a tent as the premises were not ready yet. A small airport was built to allow access to the country; the little houses that you can still see today opposite to the present ministry of rural development were built to accommodate the head of state and the members of the Government. Later on, the dispensary of Ksar was built, and then the great Mosque was constructed.

So, as you can see, five years after the independence of our country, our Capital Nouakchott, amounted to nothing but a few scattered premises with no asphalted roads, no running water, no electricity, No telephone… Moreover, the untroden bush between the existing buildings, was so thick that it still harbored a variegated wild fauna comprising snakes, hedgehogs, bush rats, hares, foxes, fennecs and even wolves and hyenas… so it was really hazardous to go from a house to another after night-fall.

This is not, however, a thorough description of what our capital used to be at its inception; it is just a rough picture meant to give you a faint idea of what this city looked like some fifty years ago. Amazing? Isn't it?

-"oh yes, it really is" said a pupil.

"How did people get drinking water since there was no running water?"

-"at first, drinking water was either welled-up from exiting boreholes or brought over in cisterns from Rosso and dolled out to the population.

And later on, the ocean water was unsalted and drunk. That of course was before the present source of Idini was discovered"

-"tell me how dangerous it really to walk the streets at night was?"

-"actually there were no streets per se, since between the few houses that existed, there was, as I was told, tall and sometimes thick bushy vegetation where wolves very often waylay passers-by especially children. Mind you, I am not telling you this just to thrill you, it is the sheer truth."

-"Gosh!! That makes my flesh creep. That must have been terribly frightening particularly for children. Isn't that so Najib" remarked another pupil.

-"yes I guess so" Najib answered smilingly. Having said this much. Najib resumed his seat after having been applauded by his fellows who seemed to have appreciated his talk about the birth of Nouakchott and its subsequent gradual growth. Then he inquired who would volunteer to talk about his or her Wilaya during the next get-together. A young lady raised her finger; she said her name was Kadia and that she was willing to talk of her Wilaya, the Gorgol, to her class-mates. Then the gathering dispersed after the pupils had taken leave from each other.

KADIA PRESENTS GORGOL

On Thursday. October the 26th, 2000, at 5p.m. the pupils met again under the same tree to resume their chit-chat. Najib invited Kadia to take the floor. She joined him and stood facing her class-mates huddled in a semi-circle in the shade of the tree. Kadia was a slim ebony-black fine-featured 16 year-old girl. She was holding a paper on which she had scribbled some notes. She shook hands with Najib and smiled to the on-looking fidgety audience trying thereby to overcome the stage-fright that made her hands slightly shake. Then she started talking:

"Ladies and gentlemen it is my pleasure to tell you something about the Wilaya I come from. This Wilaya as you all know is located in the southern part of our country, in the Senegal River valley. It is contiguous to the Wilayas of Guidimagha, Brakna, Tagant and Assaba. And it borders on the Republic of Senegal from the west. Its capital city is Kaedi and its main towns are:

Mbout, Monguel, Lekssaiba, Toufounde Cive and Maghama, which happens to be my birth place.

The yearly rainfall in the Gorgol is relatively important in relation to the other Wilayas of the country. It is also one of our most populous Wilayas. The importance of the rainfall, the humidity resulting there from, The density and the diversity of the vegetation, the availability of water and arable soils are the factors that have determined the main activities of the people in the Wilaya. These activities are first of all: agriculture which involves the traditional technique, called 'diery', consisting in growing immediately after the rainfall or on the river's banks such cereals as: millet, sorghum, maize, niebe, paddy etc… the other agricultural technique is the modern one where irrigation is systematically used. This type of agriculture allows to grow in an intensive manner: rice, cash crops… particularly fruits such as mangoes, oranges, water melons and vegetables like: carrots, tomatoes, onions, sweet potatoes, pepper, turnip etc. beside agriculture, the other main activity is cattle raising; the animals species bred in the Wilaya are: cows, sheep, goats, horse etc.: the third main activity is the river-fishing called 'walo-walo'. There are also marginal activities such as: handicraft, pottery, petty trade etc. now having told you this, I think, that to be thorough, I should mention to you the problems as will as the handicaps that do threaten the health and the social welfare of the populations of the Wilaya. These health problems are: malaria, diarrheas, guinea-worm disease, skin-affections along with cattle plagues and occasional floods. If these problems are, to a large extent, beyond the control of the populations, there are pernicious harms rooted in the traditional way of life and that people deliberately inflict on themselves; among these: scarification, female circumcisions, early marriage, and polygamy talkless of the degradation of the ecological environmental system through persistent deforestation. Yet, thanks to their dynamism and their sustained hard work, the local populations of the Gorgol, manage to get round all these handicaps; and the national authorities spare no efforts to prop up their self-help endeavors.

Well ladies and gentlemen, I am afraid this is all I can think of, for now, as far as my Wilaya is concerned. I know I have left out many worth mentioning things but we cannot always be totally exhaustive; can we? Anyway, thank you for listening and I hope I haven't bored you too much."

Najib then said: "thank you very much Kadia. Your contribution was quite insightful. There may, perhaps, be pupils who want to ask questions or make comments. Now those who have questions, please go ahead"

-"do early marriages you mentioned and early pregnancy that ensues from them have a great impact on female education? Or in other words are there many girls dropping out of school because of early marriages?"

-"of course, they do have a significant impact since the number of girls keeps thinning away as their education spirals up. As a result very few of them manage to finish their secondary education, so you see that practice has definitely a negative impact on girl education"

-"what is the attitude of educated women toward this polygamy in your Wilaya? Can you tell us about that?"

-as a matter of fact women seem to be divided toward this issue. Some are opposed to it. Others seem to be condoning it, while a third category has a wavering position vis-a-vis the question. You know this practice is so deeply imbedded in our traditions that it is very difficult to get rid of it; I for one, am opposed to it and would never put up with it but that is my personal stand nothing more."

-"what is the extent of the spread of the sexually transmitted disease, particularly AIDS in your Wilaya?"

-"I am not very well informed about these issues I must confess, but from what I hear here and there sexually transmitted diseases constitute a glaring reality nobody can ignore. Nobody can wish that reality away either. As to the existence of AIDS in the Wilaya it is undeniable but fortunately, people are becoming more and more aware of the magnitude of the danger it poses; they are therefore becoming wary…"

After the along exchange of ideas between the speaker and the audience, the debate came to an end. Najib thanked Kadia and asked the audience to give her a round of applause which it did whole- heartedly. The meeting ended and the pupils dispersed. The next get-together having been scheduled for Thursday, November 2, 2000.

SIDATY PRESENTS ASSABA

When the pupils met anew on the set date, they had to listen to a new speaker Najib had invited to address the audience. His name was Sidaty and he was from Assaba. Sidaty was a thin boy aged 15, his white skin was sun-baked, the hair of his oblong head was cut short. He had small quick moving eyes and large teeth slightly sticking out o his mouth. Sidaty stood in front of his class-metes, stared at them for a short while then said:

"Good afternoon everybody! Today it is my turn to talk to you about my Wilaya, Assaba. But first, allow me to introduce myself. My name is Sidaty; I was born in Kankossa 15 years ago. My Wilaya is, as you may well know, bordered from the west by Brakna, Gorgol and Guidimagha, from the east by Hodh El gharbi, from the north by Tagant and from the south by the Republic of Mali. Its regional capital is Kiffa. Its main towns are: Kankossa, Boumdeir. Guerou and Barkeol. The population of the Wilaya amounts to 230 000 inhabitants, its land area is 36 000 Km_. The quantity of rain that falls on the Wilaya varies from a year to another, but over the last five years it had been fairly adequate. As a result the vegetation seems to be steadily thickening and the pastures are therefore becoming greener and the grazing areas wider; all that impacts positively on the cattle breeding activity which allows a lot of people to earn their lining.

The cattle raised in the Wilaya consist essentially of camels, cows, sheep, goats and horses. The rainfall is such that it allows agriculture. Thus both traditional and modern agricultural techniques are being applied. As a result, various cereals as well as fruits and vegetables are increasingly being grown in different areas of my Wilaya. People on the other hand derive some revenues from the gathering of wild fruits such us gum Arabic and some other specific local wild fruits. Palm trees also yield a certain quantity of dates. However, Assaba is from time to time hit by natural calamities such us drought, desert locust invasions, occasional cattle plagues and some diseases like malaria, polio and children diarrhea not to mention the encroachment of the desert. But there are sustained efforts undertaken by the government to alleviate these calamitous hazards. There are indeed repeated campaigns of vaccinations both for people and for cattle. Actions are likewise being conducted to further improve the living conditions of the populace such as digging of wells, electrification of the villages, small social projects for poverty alleviation etc… having said this much, Sidaty stopped talking, scratched his head for a little while gazing at his fellows, then said: «well, I guess, I have said all that I have in mind in relation to the subject.

It would perhaps be appropriate to let you ask questions or eventually make comments. Thank you for your attention".

Najib to whom behoves the role of the debate moderator, thanked Sidaty kindly and prompted his friends to ask questions or make remarks susceptible to enrich the debate if they so wish. The pupils supplied some additional information on the Wilaya and asked a variety of questions among these the following:

-"is it true that the road leading to Kiffa is so bad that the traveler bound to that town or coming from it get some times lost to the risk of their lives?".

-"there are sections of the road that do have harassing potholes but which remain, all the same, passable while others are impaired beyond repair and this indeed compels the traveler to resort to parallel dirt-roads which are often rough and bumpy. The state of the road worsens further during the rainy season. Fortunately this road is now being totally renewed and it is expected to be perfectly passable in the very near future as I heard from many people"

-"I heard that some people in certain localities of the Wilaya refused to make use of electricity the government had brought to them, saying that is dazzles them and makes them feel dizzy. Is that true?"

-"yes there is some truth in that; you know, on account of the excessive heat that characterizes the Wilaya, people tend to stay outdoors from sun-set though sun- rise seeking the slightest cool breeze. They content themselves with the moonlight or the stars light or at any rate with the light of rustic lamps. So they did not know electricity and they did not even feel any compelling need for it. When it came to them it took them unawares and they felt, it sort of, required them to remain in-doors, which they loathed; besides they found it aggressively bright. That was why, it took them some time to adjust to it and to accept it, I think. But now, not only everybody has discovered the virtues of electricity, but hardly anybody could do without it".

-"does the old traditional practice of fattening girls by forcing them to absorb porridge or milk still exist in your Wilaya?"

-"that bad practice which is by no means specific to my Wilaya does still exist in remote areas. But it seems to be regressing now.

That horrible practice is more and more resented and denounced for it is nothing but a physical torture inflicted on helpless girls who are compelled through pinching and finger twisting, to ingurgitate food against their will, against their better judgment and at the prejudice of their health so as to hasten their body development and ultimately to hurl them into a premature marriage that would lead them to early motherhood and compel them to drop out of school and relapse into illiteracy and cretinism ".

-"its there any specific action that targets the improvement of the situation of women in the Wilaya?"

-"yes there is, the government, certain friendly countries and benevolent no-governmental organizations are joining hands to foster and help women association and cooperatives to engage into various income generating activities".

Mister Hammady, the English teacher, was intently listening to the debate going on around him, but he did not interfere with it, instead he was systematically taking note of all the information supplied and the issues raised.

When Sidaty had answered the last question asked, Najib made some closing Remarque ant set the date for the next get-together".

ISSELMOU PRESENTS TAGANT

On November the 16th 2000, the first year pupils convened to hold their third meeting as had been scheduled; the speaker Najib had to call on to take the floor that time round was a native of the Wilaya of Tagant. He was a 16 year-old boy named Isselmou. He was a reddish, round-faced, plump boy.

He was spontaneous and easy-going. He greeted his class-mates and started his talk thus: "hi, everybody! Today, it's my turn to talk to you about my Wilaya, Tagant; I hope I won't talk you asleep! Should that happen, for one never knows, I, in advance, wish you sweet dreams and kindly request you not to snort too loud! Anyway this is just to pull your leg and get over my nervousness; let me now introduce myself, my name is Isselmou, "sleilmou" for my bosom friends. I was born in 1986 in Moudjeria. I am a native of Tagant of course! This Wilaya brought under focus today, is adjacent to Adar in the north, to Brakna in the west, to

Hodh El Gharbi in the south and to Hodh El Chergui in the east. Its capital city is Tidjikja and its outstanding towns are: Tichit, Moudjria, Rachid and El Ghedia. The land area of the Wilaya is, if I am not mistaken 96.5 thousands square kilometers whereas its total population amounts to 70 000 inhabitants.

The climatic conditions that prevail in the Wilaya cause the rainfall to be rather limited and that in turn accounts for the fact that the vegetation is rather sparse, water scarce and its boring arduous and costly. The basic economic activities that such an ecological environment allows are: extensive cattle breeding and traditional agriculture. The animals reared in the Wilaya are mainly camels, cows, sheep, goats and horses. As to agriculture it involves cereals grown after the rainfall, vegetables and some fruits grown awing to irrigation; while palm trees groves in the oases of the Wilaya yield dates. Beside cattle breeding and agriculture, there is still another income-yielding activity namely: trades, for the natives of the Wilaya are reputed to have a special knack for trade. There are many successful businessmen among them who are exercising their activities all over the country.

However, the Wilaya of Tagant faces serious handicaps that are susceptible to slow down its socioeconomic development. The most challenging of these are in particular: the scarcity of water, the receding pastures. The scanty agriculture, the recurrent natural calamities like drought, cattle plagues, locust's invasions and the inexorable inching of the desert.

Notwithstanding all these factors, the Wilaya has significant assets that can be capitalized upon for a steady development; in particular the impetuous dynamism and business know-how of its natives. Besides, the integrated development of the Wilaya is under way. Thus, roads are being built to facilitate the movement of the people and the easy flow of goods; water and electricity are brought often at a high cost to the villages of the Wilaya. Social projects are being promoted to alleviate poverty; sustained action is also pursued for the eradication of illiteracy; in addition to the school enrollment rate that has already reached 90%.

The non-governmental organizations are also working in the Wilaya to help out its development. Before winding up my talk to allow for questions and remarks let me just add that given the presence in the Wilaya of ancient historic sites like Tichit, the tomb of Aboubaker ben Amer, the founder of the Al Moravid Movement, and that of the famous saint, Sidi Abdoullah Ould El haj Brahim, to mention only these, the Tagant has a virtual tourist vocation that could be developed further.

This is all I have in store for you, my friends, with respect to my Wilaya. You may which to make comments or ask questions; so I'll give you the opportunity to do so. Thank you all for your kind attention, and I am glad to see that you're still awake".

Najib requested those who wanted to take the floor to please proceed.

-"you mentioned cattle plagues and the desert encroachment as being two major problems people in Tagant have to put up with, what is being done to overcome these problems?"

-"as far as I know, there have been repeated campaigns of cattle vaccination meant to scale down and eventually to eradicate the diverse cattle plagues. As to the inching desert, there are actions aiming at stabilizing the moving dunes. Efforts for reforestation seem also to be undertaken here and there"

-"you said that the schooling rate in Tagant is 90%, have you an idea of the percentage of the schooled girls?"

-"I read in a news paper some times ago that it approaches 44%".

-"how many non-governmental organizations are operating in the Wilaya right now?"

-"there are at least a dozen of them I think. The most active of them for now ,seems to be the one called 'world vision'".

-"is it true that the wild fauna has been exterminated in Tagant because of extravagant uncontrolled hunting?"

-"I wouldn't go to that extent but I would say that if the hunting activity is better regulated as much in Tagant as in other Wilayas of the country, wild animals existence would not be as endangered as it is now"

This answer brought the debate to a close and so Najib took the floor anew to thank Isselmou for his interesting talk and requested the audience to applaud him which it did. Then the get-together was over and the pupils went home.

DIAGNA PRESENTS GUIDIMAGHA

The following meeting took place on Thursday, November the 30th, 2000, at the same place. The speaker whom Najib invited that time round to address the audience was a teen-ager named Diagna, he was a dark complexioned stout boy, aged 16 or so with a rugged face, thick lip, and a particularly flat nose. His wooly hair was coiled into tiny black-pepper-like knots. He seemed to be a bit reserved and self-conscious. When propped to start his talk, he said after a little hushed cough: "I great you all ladies en d gentlemen. To start with, let me introduce my self even if most of you do know me already. My name is Diagna; I am from the Wilaya of Guidimagha. My hometown is Diaguily which I take it must be know to all of you. I know that all of you guys know the Guidimagha's thereabouts, do you not? Even so, it won't be useless to give you precise indications concerning its geographical position.

The Wilaya of Guidimagha is located in the Senegal River valley. It is bordered by Gorgol and Assaba in the north-east and north-west, by the Republic of Senegal and that of Mali in the south-west and the south-east respectively. Its capital city is selibaby and its main towns are: Wampu, Gouraye, Khabou, Ouldyenge and Diaguily. Because of the fairly important rainfall that the Wilaya receives every year, it has a savanna type of vegetation and a more marked agricultural vocation. In fact given the relative abundance of rain, the subsequent availability of water and fertility of the soils, agriculture has always been one of the most important activities of the people of the region. Actually the Wilaya was once regarded as the granary of the country. Traditional agriculture, or dieri, which relies on old agrarian techniques, allows the growing of millet, sorghum, maize, niebe and groundnuts. Whereas the modern agriculture which applies new techniques and makes use of more sophisticated tools allows the growing of rice and even cotton. Cash crops, on the other hand, are made possible thanks to irrigation. Such a technique permits the cultivation of vegetables such as carrots, lettuce, tomatoes, sweet potatoes, pepper, beetroot onions, turnips etc.

Moreover, the existence of grassy grazing areas permits cattle breeding which is another important economic activity of Guidimagha. I should likewise mention river-fishing which is practiced by a section of the population of the Wilaya.

The other aspects of the local economy consist of wild fruits gathering, handicraft and petty trade. These are in a nutshell the staples of Guidimagha and the principal resources it is endowed with.

Another significant asset of the Wilaya consists in the hard currency remittance sent by the emigrants originating from Guidimagha who work in Europe, to their families in the different towns and villages of the region; if we add to all this the various actions undertaken by the authorities for the economic and sociocultural promotion of the Wilaya, we get an overall idea of the assets and resources of Guidimagha and its prevailing living conditions. Of course I wouldn't be thorough if I slided over the various difficulties and problems the people in Guidimagha are grappling with daily.

Among these I should state the various health hazards, the cattle plagues, the occasional natural disasters and the nefarious social practices.

Now having said this I think I`ll wind up my talk and leave room for your comments and questions; I, therefore, stand ready for your questions provided they are not too difficult".

Najib praised Diagna's talk, thanked him for his contribution, and then asked those who wanted to intervene to do so.

"You said that the remittances of the emigrants working in Europe represent an important aspect of the resources of the Wilaya. Can you tell us how those remittances contribute to the development of the local communities?"

-" the emigrants originating from the various towns and villages of Guidimagha, who work in Europe, send money back home, that money is used to build up schools, dispensaries, mosques and to drill bore holes. Funds are also raised in order to help, when need be, people to get over any unforeseen difficulties that might crop up"

-"what are the main health problems in the wilaya and how are they being coped with?"

-"the health problems the Wilaya is suffering from are similar to those prevailing in the neighboring Wilayas. Indeed there are such diseases as malaria, skin diseases, and sexually transmitted ones etc… as to the efforts made to do away with them they are undeniable but no sufficient. For now they consist in sustained actions of sensitization and campaigns of vaccination in addition to the putting in place of an increasing number of health infrastructures all over the Wilaya"

-"what about female circumcision, early marriages, polygamy and the other forms of violence against women?

Are these plights women suffer from, still as acute as ever in Guidimagha or are they abating somehow?"

-"these plights facing women are not abating yet, in fact they are still there but the awareness of the necessity of doing away with them is steadily growing and that is an elating hope many people, especially women, cling to".

After having answered all the questions his fellows asked him, Diagna ended his talk and as he did, he was applauded by the appreciative audience. Najib closed the meeting and set the date for the following one; thereupon the audience dispersed.

SOULEIMANE PRESENTS TRARZA

On Thursday, November the 30th 2000, the pupils once more convened at the same time and the same venue. When everybody got seated, Najib called upon the speaker, who was to talk about his Wilaya. His name was Souleimane and he was from the Wilaya of Trarza. Souleimane was a light-skinned adolescent. He was tall and a little bit bended forward, he had narrow shoulders and looked rather frail, but his sparkling eyes betrayed a vivid intelligence. Souleimane came forward and stood facing his class-mates. He stared at he audience for a short while then started his talk saying:

"Hi! Ladies and gentlemen. I greet you all. My name is Souleimane. I was born 16 years ago in Boutilimit. I intend to talk to you about my Wilaya, Trarza. I might miss out a detail or another, should that happen, please complement me. To begin with let me indicate the geographical location of the Wilaya.

Trarza is limited in the north by Inchiri and Adrar in the east, by Brakna.

It borders in the south on Senegal River shared by our country and the Republic of Senegal. The capital city of the Wilaya is Rosso and its main towns are: Mederdra, Boutilimit, Rkiz and Tiguint.

I think that the annual rainfall, the flora and the fauna such rainfall allows to exist, the nature and the fertility of the soil, the presence of the Senegal River and its effluents as well as the lakes and brooks that derive from it, the existence of village and towns facing each other on the two banks of the river, all these factors account for the specific socio-economic life of the Wilaya. Indeed the extended spaces with a relatively thick and various vegetation constitute grassy pastures and woody grazing areas. This is why cattle breading is a significant economic activity in the Wilaya.Besides the fertility of the soil combined with the availability of water are very propitious to all types of agriculture. we have in Trarza, as in the other Senegal river valley Wilayas, ancestral agrarian techniques consisting in cultivating cereals after the rainfall and on the river banks after the withdrawal of water, side by side with a more modern and mechanized type of agriculture on vast areas, applying new agrarian methods and utilizing sophisticated machines. These new agrarian methods characterize what is called now the modern agricultural sector, which intensively uses high-tech and performing tools. It aims at a large scale production meant to provide raw materials for local agro-industry and to export abroad.

It relies on systematic irrigation to produce such commodities as: rice, groundnut, cotton, fruits and vegetables both to meet the needs of the national market and to be exported abroad in order to earn hard currency.

Moreover, the existence of the Senegal River, its confluents and the various lakes allow a profit-yielding fishing activity. Also, the proximity of the Mauritanian villages located on the right bank of the river to the Senegalese ones facing them on the left bank, favors trade and all forms of fruitful exchanges between the people of the Wilaya and their Senegalese neighbors.

Of course like the rest of the Wilayas, Trarza faces a number of challenges such as epidemics, natural calamities, harmful social costumes etc... but people are now organizing themselves into associations, cooperatives and non-governmental organizations to better face up to these challenges; this self-help endeavor is propped up by an official policy of socio-economic promotion of the local populations. This is all I can think of, for now, in relation to the topic.

Thank you all for listening. Now I am ready for your questions. Najib thanked Souleimane for his informative talk and invited those who have observations or questions to proceed with them.

-"you spoke of the new agrarian methods of which consists the modern agriculture sector, aren't there new and modern cattle breeding methods as well? In other words haven't people started to develop intensive cattle breeding through the creation of modern ranches which could supply milk, meat, animal hides etc… to the national market?"

-"as far as I know big ranches with purposes like the ones you mentioned are not yet very many, but they are starting to appear here and there in the Wilaya and their development on a large scale should not be ruled out in the near future."

-"we know that some people of the wilaya share spiritual beliefs and worship practices with religious communities in Senegal. Does that have a significant socio-economic impact on the Wilaya?"

-"yes it does, in as much as it encourages the movement of people between the Wilaya and Senegal and by the same token it allows exchange of goods and ideas between the neighboring communities, and that ultimately implies harmony and understanding and therefore trade and all kinds of fruitful relationships".

-"is it true that the encroachment of the desert is so intense that dunes are already forming near the bank of the Senegal River?"

-"the progress of the desert towards the river is conspicuous. The town of Rosso is already invaded by moving dunes. It's really frightening! I think that drastic measures ought to be taken, and the sooner the better".

With this answer Souleimane finished his talk. Najib who was beside him, thanked him again and asked the pupils to cheer him up and that was what they did before dispersing as the meeting drew to an end.

BILAL PRESENTS BRAKNA

On Thursday December the 14th 2000, when the next meeting was held as agreed, Najib invited a boy called Bilal to acquaint his friends with his Wilaya, Brakna.

Bilal was a somehow dark-faced 16 year-old boy, he had a rather ill-kept bushy hair, but he had sympathetic eyes and a bright toothy smile. Bilal came unhurriedly forward and stood before the seated pupils, with a down cast look as he seemed to be struggling to overcome the stage-fright. He mustered his courage and said: "good afternoon everybody, my name is Bilal, I was born in 1985 in Boghe, I am here to talk to you about the Wilaya I come from namely, Brakna. My talk won't be a long and detailed lecture it will rather consist of a string of brief and even sketchy information related to the main aspect of life in the Wilaya, nothing more. To begin with let me say a word or two about its geographical position, Brakna as you are aware, is bordered from the north-west by Trarza, from the north-east by Tagant, from the south-east by Gorgol and from the south-west by Senegal.

The capital city of the Wilaya is Aleg and the main towns are: Boghe, Magtaa Lahjar and Mal.

As far as the economy of the Wilaya is conceded, one may say that it rests mainly on cattle breeding and agriculture. Indeed woody extended areas permit to raise such animals as cows, sheep and goats while the quantity of rain the Wilaya receives annually and the existence of Senegal River as well as the hinterland lakes allows agricultural activities. Thus the wide spread old agrarian methods are applied alongside small scale modern farming techniques, the gathering of local wild fruits, the river fishing, the native economic activities of the people in Brakna. All types of exchanges between the native and the Senegalese neighbours are carried out over the river to the benefit of all the parties. The populations in our Wilaya are striving to further improve their lot through the building of small dams, fire-belts and through the drilling of wells and bore holes. International NGOS and non-governmental agencies are helping out to promote better living condition for the natives. Yet in spite of all these efforts many hurdles similar to the ones existing in the other Wilayas still hinder the socio-economic advancement of the people in the region. This is all I can tell you for the time being about my home Wilaya. Now I am at your disposal for any question you may want to ask. After having commanded Bilal enlightening talk, Najib, promoted those among the audience, who wanted to intervene to go ahead.

-"is it true that the charcoal making activity is so intense in your region that it will very soon lead to a disastrous deforestation which is bound to constitute a real threat to the ecological environment in the area?" asked a member of the audience.

-"actually if Lorries loaded with charcoal is something to judge by, I can tell that that activity seems indeed be going on. To what extent it is regulated and controlled I can't tell you. I am not even sure that the local population is fully aware of the short-term danger of the deforestation caused by this activity and its devastating effect on the Wilaya. A great deal of sensitization needs still to be done to make people alive to this crucial issue I must say" remarked Bilal.

-"I heard that child mortality is still soaring in your Wilaya. How does the Wilaya fare as far as the reproduction health goes?"

-"my knowledge of these issues is based on hear-say. But I gathered that thanks to repeated vaccination campaigns

and to the multiplication of health centers all over the Wilaya, the mother and child mortality seems to be receding".

-"how are the efforts for the eradication of illiteracy going?"

-"based on what people say those efforts are still steadfastly pursued".

This having been the answer to the last question, Najib renewed his thanks for Bilal whom his friends applauded cheerfully. The meeting was thus concluded and the pupils left the school courtyard in small groups.

MARIEME PRESENTS HODH EL GHARBI

On December the 28th 2000, at a quarter to six p.m., the sixth meeting was held under the very same tree in the high-school courtyard. In his capacity as the debate moderator, Najib requested his class-mates who where loitering about to get seated so as to allow the speaker to start her talk. The speaker that time round was a 15year-old girl called Marieme, she was to talk about her Wilaya, El Hodh El Gharbi. When Najib invited Marieme to start her talk, she stepped forward taking quickly leave from two of her friends she was chatting with. She was a shortish plump girl, her fair-colored face with regular features was surrounded by abundant dark hair that flowed down her delicate shoulders. After a slight shake of her little head and as she pulled her cloth a little bit forward over her forehead she began her talk saying: "good afternoon dear fellows, I am pleased to have to talk you today about my home Wilaya, El Hodh El Gharbi, prior to that however, let me introduce my self.

My name is Marieme I am 15 year old, my birth place is Koubeni.

The Wilaya of Hodh El Gharbi we are to focus on today, stretches over 54.000 square kilometers and is bordered from the west by Assaba, from the north by Tagant, from the east by Hodh Echargui and from the south by Mali. Its capital city is Ayoun. Its main towns are: Tintane, Koubeni and Tamcheket. Its overall population is about 200.000 inhabitants. The climatic factors and the geographical configuration that characterize the Wilaya account for the type of economy it has. Indeed the volume of annual rainfall, the extended grazing spaces and the large arable lands give to the Wilaya the agro-pastoral vocation it has. Yet both agriculture and cattle raising remain traditional since they essentially rely on the old ancestral methods and techniques. These modes of extensive agriculture and cattle breeding allow the production of the same varieties of cereals that are grown in the neighboring Wilayas and the rearing of animals similar to the ones reared there. I must however say that this state of things is not likely to go on forever as very important efforts are being undertaken to modernize and promote the agro-pastoral activities in the Wilaya thanks in particular to a comprehensive and multifaceted cooperation with the German government carried out through an operator called GTZ. Such cooperation aims primarily at the modernization of the agro-pastoral sector in the Wilaya.

One should not rule out to see in the near future, the appearance in the Wilaya of an intensive exportation-oriented agriculture, as well as a new mode of cattle breading based on the ranching system aiming both at feeding downstream agro and animal industries located either in the Wilaya itself or elsewhere in the country. Another worth-mentioning aspect of the economic life of Hodh El Gharbi, consists in the various exchanges with the neighboring Republic of Mali. There are indeed intense movements of goods and people all the year long between the Wilaya and the contiguous Malian regions. One should also spell out that the large population of the Wilaya constitutes a very important human resource which if put to a good use may be an additional asset. Moreover, the supply of water and electricity to the rural communities, the putting in place of basic infrastructures such as roads, health centers, schools etc… have encouraged these communities to give up the nomadic way of life they were used to and to settle down for sedentirisation and that indeed is a qualitative change in the population's life. In spite of its significant resources, Hodh El Gharbi faces, all the same, quite a number of difficulties and problems be they ascribable to the forces of nature or to the harmful misbehavior of the populations themselves vis-a–vis their ecological environment. Well, I think that I have said what I had in pipe for you with reference to my Wilaya; therefore I'll stop here and leave room for remarks and questions.

Najib stepped forward, commanded Marieme expose and asked for comments and questions.

-" you alluded to the importance of the human resources your Wilaya is endowed with; how would you retort to those who might say that most people in your Wilaya are not keen on performing any demanding work?" asked a pupil among the audience.

-"you know the propensity to laziness and the tendency some people have to idle around rather than achieving anything good are by no means specific to the Wilaya of Hodh El Gharbi. Instead, large sections of our populations nationwide tend to have this passive attitude. Hard work and self-reliance are yet to be valued by most of us. This is why, I think, a campaign of sensitization has been, more than once, undertaken in our mass-media in order to praise perseverance and extol hard work" Marieme answered.

-"can you please tell us how important the phenomenon of women repudiation is in your Wilaya? And how it is affecting the stability of the families and the welfare of children in particular?"

-"the women repudiation as you put it or the expedious divorce as others would refer to it, is the social plague that is still afflicting our Wilaya in the same proportion as in the other parts of the country. In this respect if I am at loss to tell who ultimately bares the responsibility of this baleful practice, I am quite set as to its ruinous effects on all the members of the household it afflicts. Needless to say that the most greatly damaged victims of this thoughtless deed are undoubtedly children who are psychologically bruised and emotionally torn apart by the brutal breakdown of their families; talkless of the deprivation and the hardship they may go through on account of that breakdown… I am however glad to have heard that a law which will regulate divorces is to be promulgated very soon"

-"what is the magnitude of the rural exodus phenomenon in Hodh El Gharbi?"

-"most of young people in our Wilaya tend to flee the rural areas to go to the big towns of the country where they expect to find greater job opportunities and better living conditions. But the electrification of some of our towns and the socio-economic project aiming at the youth insertion seem to be slowing down this phenomenon".

When the pupils had asked all the questions that occurred to them, the debate came to an end, and then they dispersed after having expressed their appreciation to their class-mate's expose by a vigorous round of applause.

MOULAYE PRESENTS HODH ECHERGUI

On Thursday January the 1st 2001, by 5.30 p.m.; the first year pupils were already seated at the usual place waiting for the new speaker to show up. As Najib was asking the restless pupils to remain seated and wait for the speaker to arrive, the latter appeared suddenly; he seemed to be out of breath as he was panting. He apologized for being late. When he collected his breath, Najib invited him to start his expose without further delay. Saying: «it is my pleasure today to call on our class-mate, Moulaye to entertain us about his Wilaya, please listen to him. Go ahead Moulaye". Moulaye thanked Najib with a friendly nod. He was utterly sun-baked; his rusty hair was cut short around his ears but was left to coil over his narrow forehead. He had small eyes and a wide thin-lipped mouth. After apologizing once more for being late, he said with a slight stutter: "good afternoon dear friends I am Moulaye and I am here to talk to you about Hodh Echargui, my home Wilaya. Let me first tell you where it is.

Hodh Echergui is bordered from the north and the north-west by Adrar and Assaba, from the south-east by the Republic of Mali.

The capital city of it is Nema, of course. Its main towns are: Timbedra, which is my home town, Bassiknou, Amourj and Walata.

The Wilaya involves two distinct parts: the northern area which is dry, arid particularly, barren and the southern area which is more humid, woodier and therefore fitter for cattle raising and agriculture. The dominant mode of life in the Wilaya is nomadism;

The majority of people stall live in shiftless tent-camps. The urban centers in the Wilaya are scant, land-locked and under-populated because of the contiguity with the Republic of Mali. On account of the numerous affinities and given the relatively good neighborliness, Malian population and the people of Hodh Echargui, not only do a great deal of trade with the neighboring

Malian communities but they also cross the borders with their cattle whenever the grazing areas in the Wilaya thin away.

As a result, many natives of the Wilaya live more or less temporarily in Mali either as shepherds, brokers, petty traders or shop keepers.

As to the main problems the Wilaya suffers from, they consist in the scarcity of water and the on-going desertification.

Isolation, shiftlessness, bad health conditions, illiteracy and utter poverty are other difficulties the populations of the Wilaya are wrestling with, the meritorious efforts of the government, and those of the benevolent NGOS not withstanding; these are the aspect of my Wilaya's life that deserve to be highlighted and which I have some information on. So I'll stop here to allow you make remarks and ask questions if you so wish.

-"you mentioned a flourishing trade between Hodh Echargui in the adjacent Malian regions. What do your people sell in Mali and what do they buy from it?"

-"they essentially sell cattle, salt and sometimes green tea leaves, and they buy cereals, honey and various materials".

-" tell me, has security improved over the frontiers since the Touareg rebellion calmed down, and are there still refugees camps in Hodh Echargui?"

-"you know security over the frontiers is everybody's concern, that's why the relevant authorities of both countries do their utmost to preserve it and they succeed to a large extent to do so.

As to the presence in the Wilaya of refugee's camps, it is now less conspicuous than it used to be over the last three years".

"Is it true that girls are still being fattened and married against their will at an early age in some localities of your Wilaya?

-" you know, girl`s fattening is a deep-rooted tradition of the nomads, for whom fatness is an essential aesthetic criterion of feminine beauty; whereas thinness is regarded as disgraceful for women folk and shameful for their families; as plumpness is equated with abundance and plenty while meagerness is associated with parsimony, scarcity and stinginess. So this practice will take time to disappear all together".

-"tell me Moulaye, what is the staple food in your Wilaya? Asked a pupil smilingly.

-"it used to be a thick porridge called 'el aish' and the couscous but now rice and bread are widely consumed; Walata is one of our towns that has a very rich and variegated cuisine".

-"is it true that out there in Walata they consume a lot of hot pepper and that they even put it in their drinks?"

-"so I heard" replied Moulaye with a little laugh. This answer rounded off the talk Moulaye delivered on the Wilaya of Hodh Echargui.

Before the meeting came to an end, Najib renewed his thanks for Moulaye who was cheered up by his class-mates before they left the schoolyard in small chattering groups as the sun disappeared from the horizon.

HOURIA PRESENTS INCHIRI

The seventh get-together took place on January the 25th 2001, around 5 p.m. at the usual venue, the orator whom Najib called upon to address the audience was a female adolescent called Houria. She stepped forward unhesitatingly apparently eager to start her talk. She was a middle –sized good- looking girl with large dark eyes and a heart-shaped little mouth. She had small red pimples on her cheeks and her chin. Wasting no time, Houria started her talk thus:

"Hi everybody! My name is Houria; I am a native of Akjoujt where I was born 16 years ago. It is my pleasure to talk to you for a while about my home Wilaya, Inchiri. I'll start by indicating its geographical position in relation to the other Wilayas of the country.

Inchiri is limited from the north and the north-west by Dakhlet Nouadhibou, from the east by Adrar, and from the south by

Trarza; its capital city is Akjoujt and it has fledgling villages such as Benechab, Tamagout etc… the Wilaya of Inchiri is ill-favored in terms of rainfall,

it is therefore dry and hot, its vegetation is scanty and sparse. Water is scare and difficult to come by. Consequently the agriculture activities are marginal and cattle breeding limited and selective, since only camels sheep and goats can be reared in the region.

The resources of the Wilaya consist mainly in mineral deposits some of which had already been exploited for some times while others are being prospected for. The exploitation of the deposit of copper located in the vicinity of Akjoujt had been going on for years;

The minerals extracted there from had been refined into copper and gold. Before that deposit was completely used up, a new deposit of crude mineral deemed to be well above 23 million tons which involves 2000 tons of cobalt and 29 tons of gold, was said to have been discovered in the same area.

That deposit was expected to be exploited, thanks to a joint-venture between Australia and Mauritania which is still to flag off. Had that exploitation been carried out as expected, it would have impacted positively on the various aspect of the socioeconomic life in the Wilaya.

It is noteworthy in this connection, that many international mining companies are prospecting for gold, diamond and cobalt in the Wilaya and they are said to have come across very encouraging clues.

In terms of handicapping problems, I must point out that the Wilaya has difficulties it has to iron out whenever that is possible, if it is to clear the way for economic development. Among these are: the scanty rainfall, the scarceness of water associated with that, the dwindling grazing areas, the rampant desertification and the under- population. These are serious handicaps susceptible to hamper the undeniable dynamism of the local populations and impede the efforts of the government to speed up the economic and social promotion in the Wilaya. This, ladies and gentlemen, all I can think of telling you as far as my Wilaya goes. But I remain at your disposal for any question you think fit to ask. Najib thanked Houria for her contribution and elicited the questions and answers exchange.

-"what are the measures, if there are any that have been taken to remedy to the scarceness of water in the Wilaya?"

-"actually, if the Australian copper-exploiting company, I have mentioned earlier on, had pursued its activity in the Wilaya, it would have carried out, as agreed upon with the Mauritanian government, a steady research for water in the Wilaya.

It would have in particular built a second pipeline to carry water from Benechab to Akjoujt as well as several watering places for the cattle; unfortunately none of that had been achieved as far as I know. However, research for water and bore hole works are being relentlessly carried out by relevant national authorities in different Ares in the Wilaya as I gathered"

-"what is being done to slow down the encroachment of the desert?"

-"well, I think that the efforts undertaken in this respect are not up to the expectation. The desert keeps inexorably advancing and people do not seem to fully realize the extreme gravity of the disastrous catastrophe that is unfolding under their very eyes.

It is urgent that drastic measures be taken before everything is utterly buried".

-"do women, in your Wilaya have specific income-yielding activities?"

-"yes they definitely do. They have farming cooperatives as well as local handicraft ones. There are also feminine NGOS".

-"what is being done at the level of your Wilaya to organize the leisure time of the youth? Are there recreative activities for young people in the urban centers?"

-"to begin with, let me say that there aren't many urban centers in the Wilaya and to be honest I ought to say that there are, so far, very few recreative activities destined to the youth. Skeletal libraries and a modest cyber-café or two, are all there is in the whole Wilaya. But we do hope that this situation won't go on forever".

When all the remarks made were listened to and the questions asked answered, Najib commanded Houria's contribution once more time and had her applauded by her class-mates, then he declared the meeting closed. Upon which the pupils left the schoolyard chattering with each other.

GUEJMOUL PRESENTS TIRIS-ZEMOUR

Thursday February the 8th 2001, was the agreed deadline for the following meeting which started at 4.30 p.m., a bit early than usual. The speaker Najib had ushered in that time round was a boy named Guejmoul. He was to talk to his class-mates about his Wilaya, Tiris-Zemour. Guejmoul who bowed to his seated friends as he faced them was a thick-set adolescent aged 16 or so. He had a comely white face; his large forehead was overhung by black curly hair. He had a straight nose and fledgling moustaches. He waved his hand smilingly to salute his friends, and then said:

"Good afternoon all of you! I am pleased to have to talk to you this afternoon about Tiris-Zemour, my home Wilaya. All right, let me do like everybody did, that is to introduce my humble self even if most of you do know me already. My name is Guejmoul; I was born in Birmougrin over 16 years ago. Now let's see where Tiris-Zemour is located. This Wilaya is contiguous to Adrar, Inchiri and to the Atlantic Ocean. The regional capital of the Wilaya is Zweirat as to its main cities they are: Fderik, Birmougrein and Ain bentili.

This Wilaya is dry since it has a desert climate, and on account of its latitude, it has great thermal variations. It is very hot and dry in summer and very cold and often humid in winter.

The rainfall in the Wilaya is erratic and tardy. But when it occurs vast areas of the Wilaya turn into splendid green pastures and gorgeous flowery meadows, that's why the Wilaya has, despite its scanty rainfall a pastoral vocation all the same. It is particularly suitable for camels, sheep and goats. In addition to the animal resources, Tiris-Zemour has also mineral resources. There are indeed huge deposits of iron ore in Kidiet El Jelil, Al gallaba, El M'haoudat etc…

This mineral has been exploited and exported for decades on. Its extraction, its transportation from Zouirat to Nouadhibou and its exportation to Europe, are the responsibility of the powerful national company, SNIM-sem based in Zouirat.

This firm does actually have a great impact in terms of employment, economic development and social promotion not only on the Wilaya but on the entire country, Tiris-Zemour has its hampering handicaps; the most outstanding of which are: water scarcity, depopulation and geographical remoteness from the main urban centers of the country. However the contiguity with Morocco, Algeria and Mali is the underlying factor for the intensive exchanges between the Wilaya and the adjacent regions of these countries. These exchanges have positive fall-outs on all aspects of life in the Wilaya. Having said this, allow me to wind up my talk so as to give you the opportunity to make comments or ask questions; and thank you all for your sustained attention.

This concluding remark led Najib to step in to express his appreciation on the interesting expose Guejmoul has presented. Questions ensued, the first of which was:

"Among the difficulties facing your Wilaya, you did not mention health problems, how come?"

-"it is because there are no massive and wide spread diseases. The area is sound and healthy. There are no swamps therefore no mosquitoes and hence no malaria. There are no polluted stagnant waters; therefore there are no guinea worm affections, no large scale diarrheas and no skin diseases. As a whole the weather and the ecological environment of the Wilaya are healthier than those of the other Wilayas of the country. Mind you, this opinion might not be impartial. You can make what you like of it …" remarked Guejmoul laughingly.

-"apart from iron ore, are there other minerals in the Wilaya?"

-"it seems there are. Since many foreign companies which have sought and get permits to search for gold, diamond and other precious minerals in the Wilaya, keep renewing these permits; this could only mean that there are good reasons for them to do so".

"What is the impact of SNIM on the life of the Wilaya?"

-"first of all it provides work for a great deal of people from the Wilaya and outside it. Second it supplies water and electricity free of charge to large sections of the population particularly in Zouirat.

It also provides a valuable means of transportation for people, animals and goods all over the Wilaya. It favors sedentarization of the nomads who are keen on settling down wherever they can find water and basic commodities they need"

-"how does SNIM provide transportation to the people of the Wilaya?"

-"thanks to the train that carries iron from Zouirat to Nouadhibou and which is two kilometers long that is to say the longest train in the world; that train, in its back and forth movements carries passengers, their goods and even their cattle from a locality to another allowing thereby a steady flow of people and goods over the whole Wilaya".

When no further question was asked, Najib extolled the contribution of Gyejmoul and encouraged the audience to cheer him up, then he declared the meeting closed. The pupils left the school to go home.

SAFIA PRESENTS DAKHLET NOUADHIBOU

Thursday, February the 22th 2001, was the D-day for the penultimate meeting which was held earlier than usual since it kicked off at 4.45p.m. The pupil who was expected to present an expose on her Wilaya was a young lady named Safia.

Safia who stood beside Najib waiting for him to nod her into starting her talk, was a very pretty lass aged 16. She had a straight slim body and harmonious delicate limbs, her fair face was well shaped and her round cheeks had charming dimples. She was wearing spectacles with a fine thin golden rim that denotes a refined taste. Those spectacles were overhung by a silky black unruly forelock. When Najib gave her the nod to go ahead, she brushed aside the forelock and said as she started her talk: "good afternoon ladies and gentlemen, my name is Safia I am 16 year old and I was born in Nouadhibou. I am here today to entertain you about my Wilaya, Dakhlet Nouadhibou. I'll start, if you don't mind my pin-pointing the Wilaya on the national map so as to delineate its borders.

The Wilaya of Dakhlet Nouadhibou is contiguous to Adrar, In the north-east, to Inchiri in south-east and to the Atlantic Ocean in the west. The main localities of the Wilaya are: Boulanoir, Inal, Tmeimichat and Nouamghar. Its capital city is Nouadhibou which is the economic capital of the country as well.

The rainfall In the Wilaya is second to nothing and its dry and windy weather is congenial neither to agriculture nor to cattle raising. This is why the Wilaya has no agro-pastoral vocation what so ever.

But, deep currents that are very congenial to fish, run along its coastline. Hence its waters are among the fishiest waters the worldwide? Don't expect me though, to give you the names of the various species; that I can't do. But I can tell you that most of these fish varieties are well prized and sought after. I can also tell you that the bulk of the 400.000 tons or so of fish captured annually along our national coasts come from the coastline of the Wilaya where operate most of the domestic and foreign fleets fishing in our territorial waters and which amount to not less than 550 trawlers and 4000 small embarkations. The fishing sector, which constitutes a sizeable chunk of the national fledgling industry, involves a score of small and middle-sized companies most of which are located in Nouadhibou. The fish captured off-shore is disembarked in the fishing-port of Nouadhibou before being exported abroad. I read somewhere that the proceeds derived from the selling of fish represents a signicant proportion of the national income.

In addition to the fishing activities spearheaded by the state-owned company SMCP.

There are also mineral activities presided over by SNIM and which consist essentially of iron ore exportation from the local mineral port.

The wilaya has also a tourist vocation because of its extended beautiful beaches, its marvelous bays, its innumerable islands and its various wonderful tourist sites such as Banc d'Argin, the white cap, the seals-bay ,the Imragen villages and camps…The wilaya is also a zone of international trade, it constitutes a national gate to Europe given its closeness to Morocco and to the Canary Islands. Moreover because of the expanding international exchange carried out from Nouadhibou, there developed in the Wilaya a class of high-flying businessmen who have connections with the world markets and the international stock exchanges.

The economic and socio-cultural openness as well as the cosmopolitan vocation oh Nouadhibou will undoubtedly be enhanced by the road that is going very soon to link Dakhlet Nouadhibou to Morocco and via Morocco to Europe on the one hand and to Nouakchott and beyond Nouakchott to Senegal and black Africa on the other hand. Now as far as the weaknesses' and the shortcomings of the Wilaya are concerned they can be said to reside essentially in the scarcity of drinking water, the skyrocketing cost of life and last but not least the steady depletion of the fish resource. Let's hope that appropriate solutions will be found to these challenges in due time.

This is what I had in store for you with respect to my Wilaya, Dakhlet Nouadhibou. Now you may go ahead with remarks and questions. Najib extolled Safia informative expose and requested a round of applause for her and elicited the comments and questions.

-"you mentioned fishing and mining activities, you pointed out trade and business but you didn't say anything about cultural activities. Aren't people in your Wilaya interested in knowledge and culture?"

-"of course they are. I just forgot to mention that there are libraries, cultural centers and cyber-café in Nouadhibou thanks in particular to the praise-worthy endeavor of the town municipality to promote cultural activities in the Wilaya".

-"don't the cosmopolitan character of Nouadhibou and its being the gate of the country to Europe favor insecurity, drug trafficking and Mafiosi practices?"

-"there are risks that ought to be reckoned with. And I assume that the relevant Authorities in the Wilaya and in the country as a whole are on the lookout to prevent these evil activities".

-"are people in Dakhlet Nouadhibou, still keen on going to Las Palmas and elsewhere in Europe to spend very costly holidays during which thy squander huge amounts of hard currency the country desperately needs for its development?"

-"you know, one cannot say that all the people in the Wilaya are careless spend-thrifts but not all of them are responsible and thoughtful either. We can only hope that they will grow more and more aware of the vital necessity of the rationalized use of hard currency in a developing country like ours".

-"Tell me, are marriages decreasing in Nouadhibou as they are in Nouakchott? If so, is it because of prohibitive high dowry or is there more to it than just that, do you think?"

-"actually, I do not have handy revealing statistics concerning this issue. However based on daily observation one can't fail to notice indeed a decrease in the rate of marriages. Now how to account for this state of things? I am not sure I have a clear cut explanation. But I tend to believe that the high dowry, the long-lasting studies, the increasing difficulty for young people to find jobs, the growing unwillingness of the youth to face up to the demanding requirements of parenthood etc…

all these factors combined account perhaps for the dwindling number of marriages in our Wilaya and elsewhere in the country if not in the world at large".

This answer brought the debate to an end; after Najib has asked the audience to cheer up Safia, the gathering winds up as all the pupils departed.

MOUSTAPHA PRESENTS ADRAR

The last brought under focus was that of Adrar to which was devoted the ultimate get-together that took place on Thursday March the 8th 2001, at 5 p.m., under the same big and shady tree in the lycee courtyard. Thy English teacher who attended all the meetings was scheduled to take the floor after the last talk so as to comment on all the exposes made on to round up the significant ideas stirred up on the various relevant topics touched upon in those exposes. That was perhaps why that gathering had attracted a large number of pupils other than those of the first year.

The speaker invited by Najib to address that exceptionally crowded meeting, was 16 year-old adolescent called Moustapha, who looks to striving to get over his nervousness as he stepped forward to address the audience; he was a tall, fair-complexioned good-looking lad. He had a comely sympathetic face slightly salient cheek-bones and a rather square chin, his sparkling eyes denote a real intellectual vividness. Moustapha coughed his nervousness off and with a large smile, he said:

"dear fellows, ladies and gentlemen, I great you all and I extend special welcome to the pupils of the other classes who joined us this afternoon. My name is Moustapha and I am here to entertain you of my Wilaya, Adrar. Let me first locate it on the map. Adrar as you may not ignore is bordered from the north by Tiris-Zemour and the Republic of Mali, from the east by Hodh Echergui, from the south by Tagant and Trarza and from the west by Inchiri and Dakhlet Nouadhibou. The capital city of the Wilaya is Atar, and its main towns are: Chinguitti, Awjeft, Meddah, and last but not least Wadan, which is my hometown.

Despite the modest rainfall it receives yearly, Adrar has all the same an agro-pastoral vocation. Indeed such animals as camels, sheep and goats thrive in the Wilaya. While cereals like: wheat, burly and maize as well as vegetables and even fruits are growing in it oasis thanks to the wide-spread traditional system of irrigation. Important quantities of dates are harvested every year from the palm trees groves of the oasis. Having secular sedentary traditions, most part of the Adrar inhabitants are urbanized, methodical, hard working and thrifty. Besides the existence in the Wilaya of the famous old cities like Wadan and Chinguitti, the historic vestiges like the cites of 'Azougui', 'Tinigui' and 'Aweidir' as well as very numerous rock-drawings and such natural wonders as 'Amgjar' and 'Gelb richaf' in addition to the ever green oasis surrounded by clean sandy desert stretches bestow on the Wilaya and undeniable touristvocation.

Such a vocation is steadily being confirmed by the growing influx of European tourists who are brought over in charter flights straight from Europe to the international airport of Atar whence they go in organized trips to the different oasis either in car convoys or reading on camel backs or trekking their way to the various tourist cites in company of professional guides.

The oasis that receive important foreign tourists influx during winter time do receive another influx of people trees dates harvest period called 'Al Gueitna' which takes place every summer. Al Gueitna is a yearly occasion for commercial exchanges between Adrar and the other urban centers of the country toward which important quantities of fresh palm trees dates are exposed. A part from palm trees dates Adrar also supplies big cities of the country like Nouakchott and Nouadhibou with a wide variety of vegetables. In addition to all these assets the Wilaya seems also to have promising futures in terms of precious minerals such as diamonds and gold which are being assiduously prospected for by foreign companies. Besides the typical handicraft of the Wilaya allows a small scale production of such items as artistic palm-straw mates, colorful leather goods, hand-woven articles to state only these.

I mentioned earlier on, that the inhabitant of the Wilaya are generally speaking hard-working and thrifty, I think that I aw it to the truth to add that they are also fairly industrious and enterprising, which is why they take full advantage of the efforts the government is making all over the country to deepen the socio-economic development in all the Wilayas. They take advantage of those efforts to foster various successful business activities.

Ladies and gentlemen, this is all I have in store for you with reference to the Wilaya of Adrar and I stand ready for you comments and questions. And thank you for your sustained attention. Najib stood up, came closer to Moustapha and thanked him for his insightful talk for which the audience showed its appreciation by a lasting round of applause.

Then questions were asked the first on was this:

"you said that there are many rock-drawings sites in the Wilaya could you please be more specific about their precise locations".

-"I cannot off-handedly tell you the thereabouts of all these sites but I know for sure that there are at least to rock-drawings sites in Amagjar mountain, another one is located just after the pass of Nouatil of the road of Chinguitti.

There are nine rock-drawing sites in Wadan and this thereabouts, some of which are in caves while others are in the open air. Three other sites are located in places called 'Gelb El beyid', 'akweike' and 'sbil' respectively at 80 KM, 152 KM and 160 KM north of Wadan".

-"is it true that the Portuguese had settled down in Wadan for some time in the remote past? If so. When was that and what was it for?"

-"as far as I know, the Portuguese did not settle down in the city of Wadan per se; they rather built a factory for trade in a place known now as 'Agueidir ' at 25 KM north of Wadan and that was 15th century it was precisely in 1487, as I read in a history book sometimes ago. They settled around that factory for more than 7 years during which they traded with the natives of Wadan which was then a very prosperous city".

-"does that mean that the Portuguese had somehow participated in building of Wadan?"

-"no it does not. Actually if what I read is accurate, when the Portuguese settled down near Wadan, the city had already been existing for three centuries, since it had been founded in 536 ano Hegira corresponding to 1142 ano Domini"

-"tell me what tourists seek in Adar? What are they attracted to in there?"

-"I do not know exactly. Bu what I can tell you is that they seem to enjoy very much riding camels in the vast clean sandy desert. They also appear to be very fond of spending night in tent-camps in the company of nomads contemplating the starry sky and listening, so to speak, to utter silence. That indeed seems to be an experience they found unique and therefore worth their will. And that is the opinion of the horse as people say".

-"you mentioned more than once the laborious character of the people of Adrar what does that character consist in? Can you expatiate a little bit?"

-"it consist in the fact that neither men nor women loath strenuous work besides they do not shy away from any income yielding activity. That was what I based my assertion on"

-"is it true that the Wilaya has a refined cuisine?"

-"I believe so. If what the non-native say is something on can judge by, the specific dishes of the Wilaya are very well appreciated specially the variety of 'couscous' made up of a mixture of local wheat and barley flour; talkless of the Wadan thin pan-cakes called 'lekssour' made up of the same flour".

This concluded the discussion that ensued from the expose delivered by Moustapha on Adrar.

Najib expressed his appreciation for such an expose and prompted the audience to give its author a warm round of applause which it an unhesitatingly did.

This being the last of the series of talks concerning the different Wilayas of the country, Najib invited mister Hammadi, the English teacher to make the concluding remarks and to assess that experience that had been going on for several weeks.

HAMMADI PRESENTS MAURITANIA

Mister Hammadi stood up and said with a friendly smile: "drear pupils, my friends, good afternoon. To start with let me congratulate all of you for the unflagging steadfastness you have displayed throughout these weeks. I also want to command strongly the remarkable efforts made by those of you who have presented exposes related to their respective Wilayas. And above all, I should like to extend a special thank to your class-mate, Najib for his bright idea to organize these very fruitful get-togethers. This meritorious idea has led to an original experience which would hopefully evolve into a permanent and institutionalized format such as a youth center or a debating club or something of this kind; specially that the prevailing contest is characterized by a policy of keen benevolence toward knowledge, culture and communication.

As far as the exposes presented are concerned, they have indeed shed light on the specificities of our different Wilayas, they have likewise underscored the various handicaps that constitute stumbling blocks in the way of the development of each one of these Wilayas.

They had equally pin-pointed the peculiar challenges each Wilaya has to face up to as well as the pernicious socio-cultural practices that ought to be urgently remedied to, such as:

-utter neglect of hygiene

-fattening of girls

-early marriages

-abusive divorce

-polygamy

-high dowries

-mutilating practices inflicted on girls

-laziness

-deforestation and destruction of the wild life etc…

Neither did the exposes overlook the praiseworthy efforts, the government, the friendly countries the non-governmental organizations and the civil society are making in all the wilayas in order to improve the living conditions of the populations in terms of health, education, poverty alleviation and so on.

Those are the most salient aspect your thought-provoking talks have brought under sharp focus.

Now having said this let me complement what the various speakers have come up with in their respective talks. Our country which is as you know at the same time the sum total of our

Wilayas and something more, is encompassed between the southern part of the Arab Maghreb and the northern part of the Sudamo-Sahelian zone, and it is consequently subjected to a dry hot climate in the north where the average rainfall hardly reaches 63mm and to a hot moist climate of Sahelian type in the south where the yearly rainfall reaches 600 to 650mm. the rainfall is determined by the trade winds which cause the rainy season to extend from July through September.

The land area of the country is as you know 1.030.700 square kilometers on which live 2,8 million inhabitants. 52,4% of our population are now stabilized. Its annual rate of growth is 2,6%/ life expectancy is 45 years.

The country has a coastline of 750 kilometers. Although Mauritania is endowed with various animal and natural resources such as: cattle, fish, iron, ore, copper, gold, gypsum, phosphate etc...

it has so far been rated as a poor country since its annual average income per capita is around 480 US dollars.

Until 1985, the country was in a very tight economic situation.

The weight of the indebtedness was smashing; the rate of the economic growth was second to nothing.

The inflation was soaring, the trade deficit was deepening. In a word all the economic indicators were alarming indeed. But as of 1986 deep reaching successive economic reforms were undertaken. They consisted in a series of complementary structural adjustment programs. These reforms which fostered economic liberalism were propped up by radical political transformations which had culminated in the instauration of grass-root democracy and the rule of law that had in turn brought about a socio-cultural mutation. Consequently, the rate of growth of our national economy spiraled up, the inflation decreased and all the deficits were gradually brought under control. This qualitative leap forward had strengthened the confidence of the financial institutions into our country and increased its credibility on the international plan. All that had, over the years, led to the gradual cancellation of the foreign debt owed by the country loosening thereby the strong pressure it was submitted to.

As a result, the country has begun to have cash surplus which is now being invested in a wide span of national project bearing on agriculture, health, education etc…

the enlarged investment capacity of the country allowed the latter to earmark important funds to finance not only the main infrastructures it needs in the short and medium terms but also the national strategy for poverty alleviation which aims among other things at bringing the rate of poverty to less than 17% and that of illiteracy to 21% of the global population by the year 2015.

All in all what everyone of us should clearly understand is that the national strategy consisting in: the eradication of illiteracy, the alleviation of poverty, the integration of women in the economic process, the up-grading of the national system of education, the radicalization of the economic liberalism, the entrenchment of democracy and the institutionalization of good governance aims among other things at setting the stage for the coming globalization and therefore at increasing the preparedness of the country to the challenging competition the globalization is unavoidably bound to usher in and which could be likened to an economic and cultural Darwinism where only the fittest nations will survive while the weakest will, sooner than later, be left in the cold.

This is why all the generations of this country including yourself, of course, should join hands not only to allow Mauritania to survive but also to make it thrive and to hoist it to a honorable rank among the nations of the world.

Once again I thank you for your undivided attention and god bless us all.

When mister Hammadi finished his intervention, Najib took the floor to thank him warmly on behalf of all his class-mates who spontaneously rise to cheer up their teacher giving him a standing ovation before they all departed fully satisfied with this rewarding experience of theirs, which allowed them to learn a great deal about their country, Mauritania.

L'HARMATTAN ITALIE
Via Degli Artisti 15; 10124 Torino

L'HARMATTAN HONGRIE
Könyvesbolt ; Kossuth L. u. 14-16
1053 Budapest

L'HARMATTAN BURKINA FASO
Rue 15.167 Route du Pô Patte d'oie
12 BP 226 Ouagadougou 12
(00226) 76 59 79 86

ESPACE L'HARMATTAN KINSHASA
Faculté des Sciences sociales,
politiques et administratives
Université de Kinshasa
BP243, KIN XI

L'HARMATTAN CONGO
67, av. E. P. Lumumba
Bât. – Congo Pharmacie (Bib. Nat.)
BP2874 Brazzaville
harmattan.congo@yahoo.fr

L'HARMATTAN GUINÉE
Almamya Rue KA 028, en face du restaurant Le Cèdre
OKB agency BP 3470 Conakry
(00224) 60 20 85 08
harmattanguinee@yahoo.fr

L'HARMATTAN CÔTE D'IVOIRE
M. Etien N'dah Ahmon
Résidence Karl / cité des arts
Abidjan-Cocody 03 BP 1588 Abidjan 03
(00225) 05 77 87 31

L'HARMATTAN MAURITANIE
Espace El Kettab du livre francophone
N° 472 avenue du Palais des Congrès
BP 316 Nouakchott
(00222) 63 25 980

L'HARMATTAN CAMEROUN
BP 11486
Face à la SNI, immeuble Don Bosco
Yaoundé
(00237) 99 76 61 66
harmattancam@yahoo.fr

L'HARMATTAN SÉNÉGAL
« Villa Rose », rue de Diourbel X G, Point E
BP 45034 Dakar FANN
(00221) 33 825 98 58 / 77 242 25 08
senharmattan@gmail.com

Achevé d'imprimer par Corlet Numérique - 14110 Condé-Sur-Noireau
N° d'imprimeur : 78714 - Dépôt légal : avril 2011 - *Imprimé en France*